THAT'S STRANGE!

THE HAUNTING OF BELL WITCH

Tom Jackson

Lerner Publications ◆ Minneapolis

Copyright © 2025 by Lerner Publishing Group, Inc.

All rights reserved. International copyright secured. No part of this book may be reproduced, stored in a retrieval system, or transmitted in any form or by any means—electronic, mechanical, photocopying, recording, or otherwise—without the prior written permission of Lerner Publishing Group, Inc., except for the inclusion of brief quotations in an acknowledged review.

Lerner Publications Company
An imprint of Lerner Publishing Group, Inc.
241 First Avenue North
Minneapolis, MN 55401 USA

For reading levels and more information, look up this title at www.lernerbooks.com.

Main body text set in ITC Franklin Gothic.
Typeface provided by International Typeface Corporation.

Library of Congress Cataloging-in-Publication Data

Names: Jackson, Tom, 1972–author.
Title: The haunting of Bell Witch / Tom Jackson.
Description: Minneapolis : Lerner Publications, [2025] | Series: That's strange! UpDog Books | Includes bibliographical references and index. | Audience: Ages 8–11 | Audience: Grades 4–6 | Summary: "The Bell family thought they were being haunted. For three years, an angry ghost bothered them. It finally stopped after the father died. Did the ghost kill him? Readers will learn about the Bell Witch"—Provided by publisher.
Identifiers: LCCN 2024015157 (print) | LCCN 2024015158 (ebook) | ISBN 9798765648179 (lib. bdg.) | ISBN 9798765662519 (pbk.) | ISBN 9798765659038 (epub)
Subjects: LCSH: Ghosts—Tennessee—Robertson County—Juvenile literature. | Poltergeists—Tennessee—Robertson County—Juvenile literature. | Bell family—Juvenile literature.
Classification: LCC BF1473.B37 J33 2025 (print) | LCC BF1473.B37 (ebook) | DDC 133.1/29768464—dc23/eng/20240508

LC record available at https://lccn.loc.gov/2024015157
LC ebook record available at https://lccn.loc.gov/2024015158

Manufactured in the United States of America

1 – CG – 12/15/24

Table of Contents

On the Farm 4

A Ghost is Here 10

Meeting the Witch 18

A Killer Ghost? 22

Glossary 30

Check It Out! 31

Index 32

On the Farm

The Bell family lived in Tennessee two hundred years ago.

Plow

The family were farmers.

In 1817, John Bell said he saw unusual creatures around the farm.

Soon after, the house was filled with noises.

The Bell family thought there was a ghost.

UP NEXT!

A TALKING SPIRIT!

A Ghost is Here

The Bell family said they heard a woman's voice in the house.

She said she was a spirit and she was unhappy.

Family members said that something pulled their hair.

Sometimes they heard the witch threaten John Bell.

The Bells' story became known as the Bell Witch.

Ghost hunters wanted to see the witch.

UP NEXT!

MORE HAUNTINGS.

List Break!

Famous ghosts
Ghosts are not real but there are many stories about them.

- The Headless Horseman is said to ride on the road near Sleepy Hollow, New York.

- Bloody Mary is said to appear in a mirror if someone says her name three times!

- **The *Flying Dutchman* is a ghost ship seen at sea as a warning of disaster.**

Meeting the Witch

Local people said they were being haunted too.

One man said he met a dog with two heads!

A family friend said he grabbed the witch in a bedsheet.

He dropped it because it was so heavy and smelly!

UP NEXT!

SOMEONE DIES.

A Killer Ghost?

The family was under attack for three years.

John Bell became very ill.

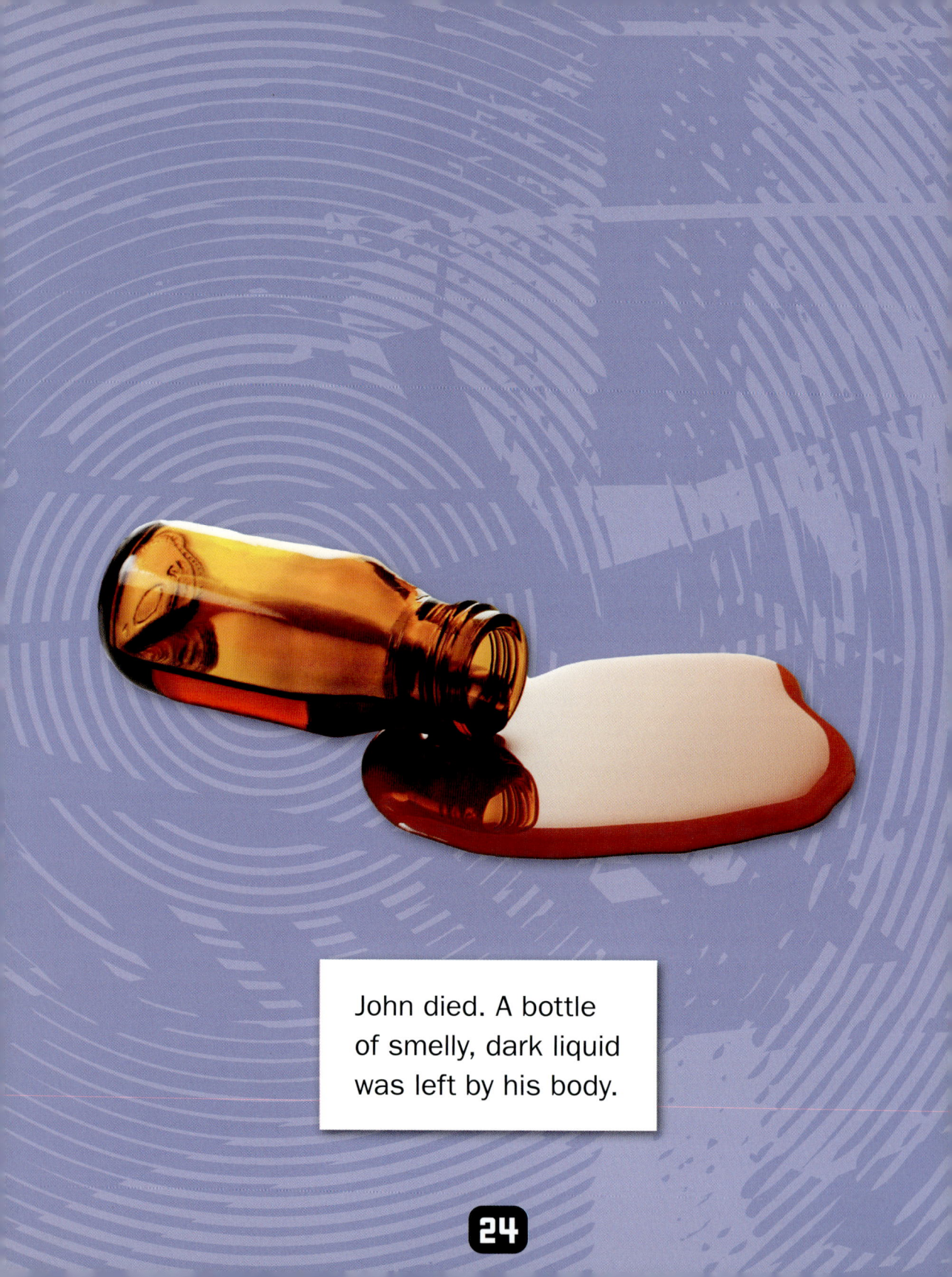

John died. A bottle of smelly, dark liquid was left by his body.

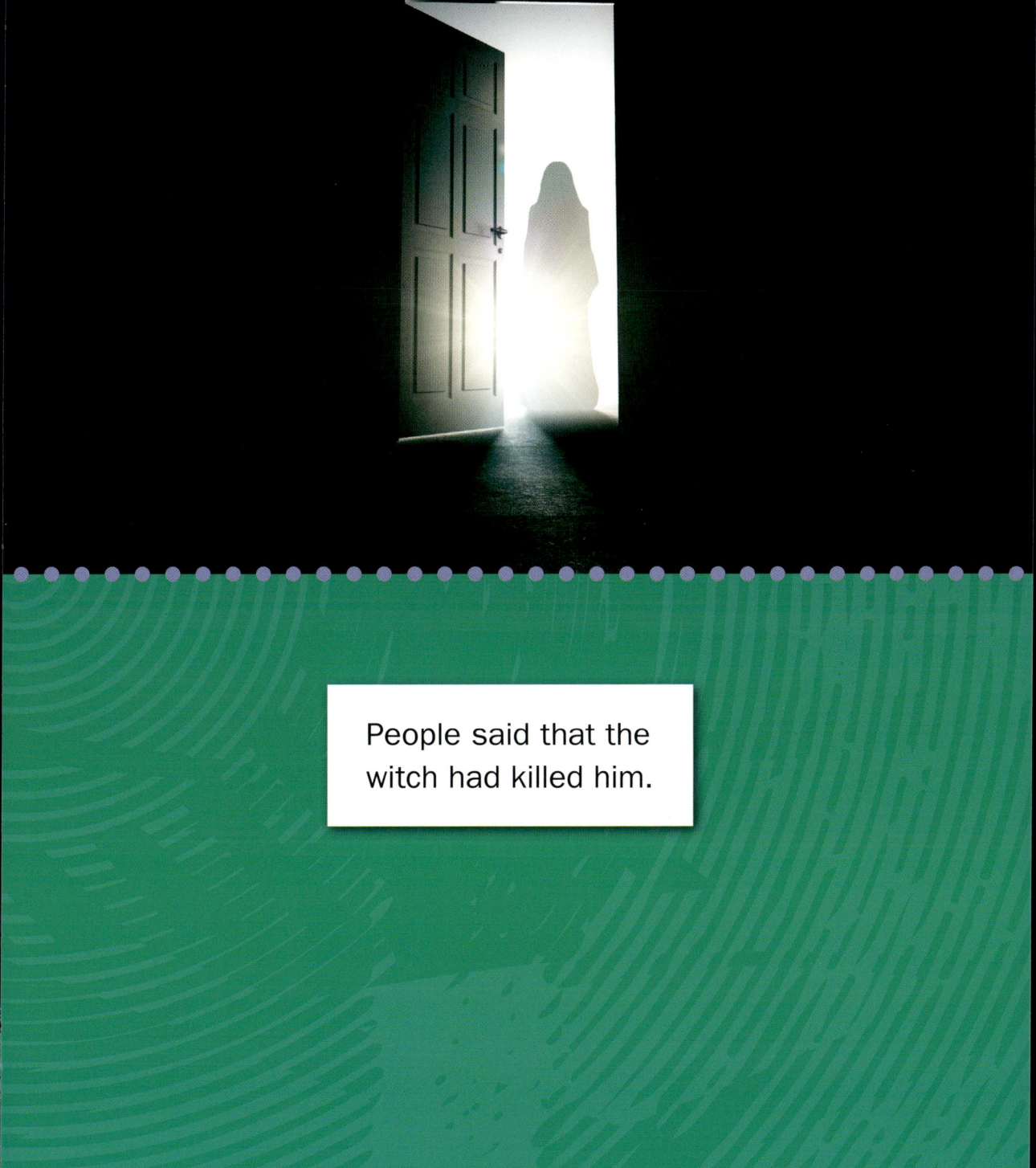

People said that the witch had killed him.

The haunting stopped after John died.

But some say the Bell Witch still lives in a cave nearby!

Modern scientists think that John was poisoned with arsenic.

If it wasn't the Bell Witch, then who was the real killer?

Glossary

arsenic: a poisonous chemical with a strong smell

haunt: when a ghost is said to be near

liquid: a runny substance, like water

poison: a chemical that hurts you

Check It Out!

Britannica Kids: Ghost
https://kids.britannica.com/kids/article/ghost/574605

Hoena, B. A. *The Bell Witch Haunting*. Minneapolis: Bellwether Media, Inc., 2020.

Katz, Susan B. *Famous Ghosts*. Minneapolis: Lerner Publications, 2024.

Kiddle: Bell Witch Cave Facts for Kids
https://kids.kiddle.co/Bell_Witch_Cave

Kiddle: Ghost Facts for Kids
https://kids.kiddle.co/Ghost

Rose, Rachel. *Frightening Farms*. Minneapolis: Bearport Publishing Company, 2021.

Index

cave, 27

dog, 19

ghost, 9, 16–17

poison, 28

Tennessee, 4

witch, 13, 14–15, 18, 20, 25, 27, 29

Photo Acknowledgments

Image credits: Gareth Howlett/Shutterstock, pp. 3, 23; Natwick/Shutterstock, pp. 4–5; Everett Collection/Shutterstock, pp. 6, 18; Raggedstione/Shutterstock, pp. 7, 15, 16 (bottom); Kiselev Andrey Valerevich/Shutterstock, p. 8; Tom Tom/Shutterstock, p. 9; Neil Lockhart/Shutterstock, p. 10; Daniel Tudorache/Shutterstock, p. 11; Teguh Pramadita/Shutterstock, p. 12; Bundit Yuwannasiri/ Shutterstock, p. 13; Mimadeo/Shutterstock, p. 14; Elena Korobeynikova/Shutterstock, p. 16(top); welburnstuart/Shutterstock, p. 17; Yusup ahmad/Shutterstock, p. 19; Lario Tus/Dreamstime.com, p. 20; Natdanai99/Shutterstock, p. 21; Altitudevs/Dreamstime.com, p. 22; Ground Pictures/Shutterstock, p. 23; Studio Araminta/Shutterstock, p. 24; Lario Tus/Shutterstock, p. 26; Www78/Wikimedia Commons, p. 27; Bob Pool/Shutterstock, p. 29; Design elements: sokolovski/Shutterstock, pp. 1–32.

Cover: sokolovski/Shutterstock; Mddi Avery/Shutterstock; Rainbowchaser/Dreamstime.com.